P9-BJS-309

All-Time Favorite
Best Casseroles

Chicken-Asparagus Casserole

Makes 12 servings

- 2 teaspoons vegetable oil
- 1 cup seeded and chopped green and/or red bell peppers
- 1 medium onion, chopped
- 2 cloves garlic, minced
- 1 can (10¾ ounces) condensed cream of asparagus soup
- 1 container (8 ounces) ricotta cheese
- 2 cups (8 ounces) shredded Cheddar cheese, divided
- 2 eggs
- 1½ cups chopped cooked chicken
- 1 package (10 ounces) frozen chopped asparagus,* thawed and drained
- 8 ounces egg noodles, cooked
- Black pepper (optional)

*Or, substitute ½ pound fresh asparagus cut into ½-inch pieces. Bring 6 cups water to a boil over high heat in large saucepan. Add fresh asparagus. Reduce heat to medium. Cover and cook 5 to 8 minutes or until crisp-tender. Drain.

1. Preheat oven to 350°F. Grease 13×9-inch casserole; set aside.

2. Heat oil in small skillet over medium heat. Add bell peppers, onion and garlic; cook and stir until vegetables are crisp-tender.

3. Mix soup, ricotta cheese, 1 cup Cheddar cheese and eggs in large bowl until well blended. Add onion mixture, chicken, asparagus and noodles; mix well. Season with pepper, if desired.

4. Spread mixture evenly in prepared casserole. Top with remaining 1 cup Cheddar cheese.

5. Bake 30 minutes or until center is set and cheese is bubbly. Let stand 5 minutes before serving. Garnish as desired.

Chicken-Asparagus Casserole

Spaghetti Pie

Makes 6 servings

- 4 ounces uncooked thin spaghetti
- 1 egg
- ¼ cup grated Parmesan cheese
- 1 teaspoon Italian seasoning
- ⅔ cup reduced-fat ricotta cheese
- ½ pound 93% lean ground turkey
- 1 teaspoon chili powder
- ¼ teaspoon crushed fennel seeds
- ¼ teaspoon black pepper
- ⅛ teaspoon ground coriander
- 1 can (14½ ounces) diced tomatoes, undrained
- 1½ cups sliced fresh mushrooms
- 1 cup chopped onion
- 1 can (8 ounces) tomato sauce
- ¼ cup tomato paste
- 1 clove garlic, minced
- 2 teaspoons dried basil leaves
- 1 cup (4 ounces) shredded part-skim mozzarella cheese

1. Cook spaghetti according to package directions, omitting salt. Drain and rinse well under cold water until pasta is cool; drain well.

2. Beat egg, Parmesan cheese and Italian seasoning lightly in medium bowl. Add spaghetti; blend well. Spray deep 9-inch pie plate with nonstick cooking spray. Place spaghetti mixture in pie plate. Press onto bottom and up side of pie plate. Spread ricotta cheese on spaghetti layer.

3. Preheat oven to 350°F. Combine turkey, chili powder, fennel seeds, pepper and coriander in medium bowl. Spray large nonstick skillet with nonstick cooking spray; heat over medium heat until hot. Brown turkey mixture until turkey is no longer pink, stirring to break up meat. Add remaining ingredients except mozzarella cheese. Cook and stir until mixture boils. Spoon mixture over ricotta cheese in pie plate.

4. Cover pie plate with foil. Bake 20 minutes. Remove foil. Sprinkle with mozzarella cheese; bake 5 minutes or until cheese is melted. Cut into 6 wedges and serve.

Spaghetti Pie

Country Sausage Macaroni and Cheese

Makes 6 to 8 servings

- 1 pound BOB EVANS® Special Seasonings Roll Sausage
- 1½ cups milk
- 12 ounces pasteurized processed Cheddar cheese, cut into cubes
- ½ cup Dijon mustard
- 1 cup diced fresh or drained canned tomatoes
- 1 cup sliced mushrooms
- ⅓ cup sliced green onions
- ⅛ teaspoon cayenne pepper
- 12 ounces uncooked elbow macaroni
- 2 tablespoons grated Parmesan cheese

Preheat oven to 350°F. Crumble and cook sausage in medium skillet until browned. Drain on paper towels. Combine milk, processed cheese and mustard in medium saucepan; cook and stir over low heat until cheese melts and mixture is smooth. Stir in sausage, tomatoes, mushrooms, green onions and cayenne pepper. Remove from heat.

Cook macaroni according to package directions; drain. Combine hot macaroni and cheese mixture in large bowl; toss until well coated. Spoon into greased shallow 2-quart casserole dish. Cover and bake 15 to 20 minutes. Stir; sprinkle with Parmesan cheese. Bake, uncovered, 5 minutes; let stand 10 minutes before serving. Refrigerate leftovers.

Fish Broccoli Casserole

Makes 4 servings

- 1 package (10 ounces) frozen broccoli spears, thawed
- 1 cup cooked flaked Florida whitefish
- 1 can (10¾ ounces) condensed cream of mushroom soup
- ½ cup milk
- ¼ teaspoon salt
- ⅛ teaspoon freshly ground black pepper
- ½ cup crushed potato chips

Preheat oven to 425°F. Grease 1½-quart casserole. Layer broccoli in prepared casserole. Combine fish, soup, milk, salt and pepper in large bowl. Spread fish mixture over broccoli. Sprinkle with potato chips. Bake 12 to 15 minutes or until golden brown.

*Favorite recipe from **Florida Department of Agriculture and Consumer Services, Bureau of Seafood and Aquaculture***

Country Sausage Macaroni and Cheese

Pesto Lasagna

Makes 8 servings

  1 package (16 ounces) uncooked lasagna noodles
  3 tablespoons olive oil
 1½ cups chopped onion
  3 cloves garlic, finely chopped
  3 packages (10 ounces each) frozen chopped spinach,
      thawed and squeezed dry
    Salt
    Black pepper
  3 cups (24 ounces) ricotta cheese
 1½ cups prepared pesto sauce
  ¾ cup (3 ounces) grated Parmesan cheese
  ½ cup pine nuts, toasted
  6 cups (16 ounces) shredded mozzarella cheese
    Red pepper strips (optional)

1. Preheat oven to 350°F. Oil 13×9-inch casserole or lasagna pan. Partially cook lasagna noodles according to package directions.

2. Heat oil in large skillet. Cook and stir onion and garlic until transparent. Add spinach; cook and stir about 5 minutes. Season with salt and pepper. Transfer to large bowl.

3. Add ricotta cheese, pesto, Parmesan cheese and pine nuts to spinach mixture; mix well.

4. Layer 5 lasagna noodles, slightly overlapping, in prepared casserole. Top with ⅓ of spinach-ricotta mixture and ⅓ of mozzarella cheese. Repeat layers twice.

5. Bake about 35 minutes or until hot and bubbly. Garnish with red pepper strips, if desired.

Pesto Lasagna

Easy Vegetable Beef Stew

Makes 4 servings

- 1 **pound beef for stew, cut into 1-inch pieces**
- 1 **can (14½ ounces) diced tomatoes, undrained**
- 1 **medium onion, cut into 8 wedges**
- 4 **carrots, cut into 1-inch pieces**
- 1 **green or red bell pepper, diced**
- 1 **rib celery, sliced**
- 1 **teaspoon Italian seasoning**
- ½ **teaspoon salt**
- ½ **teaspoon black pepper**
- 1 **tablespoon vegetable oil**
- 1 **package (8 ounces) sliced mushrooms**

1. Preheat oven to 325°F. Combine beef pieces, tomatoes with juice and onion in Dutch oven. Cover tightly; bake 1 hour.

2. Add carrots, bell pepper, celery, Italian seasoning, salt and black pepper to beef mixture; stir. Cover; bake an additional 45 minutes or until beef and carrots are tender.

3. Heat oil in large skillet over medium heat. Add mushrooms; cook and stir 10 minutes or until lightly browned and tender. Stir mushrooms into beef stew. Adjust seasonings to taste.

Variation: Two unpeeled medium red potatoes, cut into 2-inch pieces, may be added with carrots.

Lit'l Smokies 'n' Macaroni 'n' Cheese

Makes 8 servings

- 1 **package (7 ¼ ounces) macaroni and cheese mix, prepared according to package directions**
- 1 **pound HILLSHIRE FARM® Lit'l Smokies**
- 1 **can (10 ¾ ounces) condensed cream of celery or mushroom soup, undiluted**
- ⅓ **cup milk**
- 1 **tablespoon minced parsley (optional)**
- 1 **cup (4 ounces) shredded Cheddar cheese**

Preheat oven to 350°F.

Combine prepared macaroni and cheese, Lit'l Smokies, soup, milk and parsley, if desired, in medium bowl. Pour into small greased casserole. Sprinkle Cheddar cheese over top. Bake, uncovered, 20 minutes or until heated through.

Easy Vegetable Beef Stew

Mini Chicken Pot Pies

Makes 8 servings

1	container (about 16 ounces) refrigerated reduced-fat buttermilk biscuits
1½	cups milk
1	package (1.8 ounces) white sauce mix
2	cups cut-up cooked chicken
1	cup frozen assorted vegetables, partially thawed
2	cups shredded Cheddar cheese
2	cups *French's*® French Fried Onions

1. Preheat oven to 400°F. Separate biscuits; press into 8 (8-ounce) custard cups, pressing up sides to form crust.

2. Whisk milk and sauce mix in medium saucepan. Bring to boiling over medium-high heat. Reduce heat to medium-low; simmer 1 minute, whisking constantly, until thickened. Stir in chicken and vegetables.

3. Spoon about ⅓ cup chicken mixture into each crust. Place cups on baking sheet. Bake 15 minutes or until golden brown. Top each with cheese and French Fried Onions. Bake 3 minutes or until golden.

Prep Time: 15 minutes
Cook Time: about 20 minutes

Easy Chicken Chalupa

Makes 6 servings

1	roasted chicken (about 2 pounds)
12	flour tortillas
2	cups reduced-fat shredded Cheddar cheese
1	cup mild green chili salsa
1	cup mild red salsa

1. Preheat oven to 350°F. Spray large ovenproof dish with cooking spray.

2. Remove chicken meat from bones and shred. Discard bones and skin.

3. Lay 1 or 2 tortillas in bottom of baking dish, overlapping slightly. Layer tortillas with chicken, cheese and salsas. Repeat layers until baking dish is full. Finish with cheese and salsas.

4. Bake casserole 25 minutes or until bubbly and hot.

Tip: Serve with low-fat sour cream, chopped cilantro, sliced black olives, sliced green onions and sliced avocado.

Mini Chicken Pot Pies

Caribbean Black Bean Casserole with Spicy Mango Salsa

Makes 6 servings

- 2 **cups chicken broth**
- 1 **cup uncooked basmati rice**
- 2 **tablespoons olive oil, divided**
- ½ **pound chorizo sausage**
- 2 **cloves garlic, minced**
- 1 **cup chopped red bell pepper**
- 3 **cups canned black beans, rinsed and drained**
- ½ **cup chopped fresh cilantro**
- 2 **small mangoes**
- 1 **cup chopped red onion**
- 2 **tablespoons honey**
- 2 **tablespoons white wine vinegar**
- 1 **teaspoon curry powder**
- ½ **teaspoon salt**
- ½ **teaspoon ground red pepper**

1. Place chicken broth in medium saucepan. Bring to a boil over high heat; stir in rice. Reduce heat to low; simmer, covered, 20 minutes or until liquid is absorbed and rice is tender.

2. Heat 1 tablespoon oil in heavy, large skillet over medium heat. Add sausage; cook, turning occasionally, 8 to 10 minutes until browned and no longer pink in center. Remove from skillet to cutting surface. Cut into ½-inch slices; set aside. Drain fat from skillet.

3. Preheat oven to 350°F. Grease 1½-quart casserole; set aside. Add remaining tablespoon oil to skillet; heat over medium-high heat. Add garlic; cook and stir 1 minute. Add bell pepper; cook and stir 5 minutes. Remove from heat. Stir in beans, sausage, rice and cilantro.

4. Spoon sausage mixture into prepared casserole; cover with foil. Bake 30 minutes or until heated through.

5. Meanwhile, peel mangoes; remove seeds. Chop enough flesh to measure 3 cups. Combine mango and remaining ingredients in large bowl.

6. Serve casserole with mango salsa.

Caribbean Black Bean Casserole with Spicy Mango Salsa

Chicken Cassoulet

Makes 6 servings

- 4 **slices bacon**
- ¼ **cup all-purpose flour**
  Salt and black pepper
- 1¾ **pounds chicken pieces**
- 2 **cooked chicken sausages, cut into ¼-inch pieces**
- 1 **onion, chopped**
- 1½ **cups diced red and green bell pepper (2 small bell peppers)**
- 2 **cloves garlic, finely chopped**
- 1 **teaspoon dried thyme leaves**
  Olive oil
- 2 **cans (about 15 ounces each) white beans, such as Great Northern, rinsed and drained**
- ½ **cup dry white wine (optional)**

1. Preheat oven to 350°F. Cook bacon in large skillet over medium-high heat until crisp. Remove and drain on paper towels. Cut into 1-inch pieces.

2. Pour off all but 2 tablespoons fat from skillet. Place flour in shallow bowl; season with salt and black pepper. Dip chicken pieces in flour; shake off excess and brown in batches over medium-high heat in skillet. Remove and set aside. Lightly brown sausages in same skillet. Remove and set aside.

3. Add onion, bell peppers, garlic, thyme, salt and black pepper to skillet. Cook and stir over medium heat about 5 minutes or until softened. Add olive oil as needed to prevent sticking. Transfer to 13×9-inch baking dish. Add beans; mix well. Top with chicken, sausages and bacon. If desired, add wine to skillet; cook and stir over medium heat, scraping up brown bits. Pour over casserole.

4. Cover; bake 40 minutes. Uncover and bake 15 minutes more or until chicken is no longer pink in center.

Chicken Cassoulet

Sunny Day Casserole

Makes 6 servings

- 1 jar (8 ounces) pasteurized processed cheese spread, melted
- ¾ cup milk
- 4 cups diced potatoes, partially cooked
- 2 cups diced HILLSHIRE FARM® Ham
- 1 package (16 ounces) frozen mixed vegetables, thawed
- ½ cup chopped onion
- 1 cup (4 ounces) shredded Swiss, Cheddar or Monterey Jack cheese
- 1 cup cracker crumbs

Preheat oven to 350°F.

Combine cheese spread and milk in large bowl. Stir in potatoes, Ham, mixed vegetables and onion. Pour into medium casserole. Bake, covered, 45 minutes, stirring occasionally. Sprinkle Swiss cheese and cracker crumbs over top. Bake, uncovered, until Swiss cheese is melted.

Rigatoni Con Ricotta

Makes 12 servings

- 1 package (16 ounces) BARILLA® Rigatoni
- 2 eggs
- 1 container (15 ounces) ricotta cheese
- ¾ cup (3 ounces) grated Parmesan cheese
- 1 tablespoon dried parsley
- 2 jars (26 ounces each) BARILLA® Lasagna & Casserole Sauce or Marinara Pasta Sauce, divided
- 3 cups (12 ounces) shredded mozzarella cheese, divided

1. Preheat oven to 375°F. Spray 13×9×2-inch baking pan with nonstick cooking spray. Cook rigatoni according to package directions; drain.

2. Beat eggs in small bowl. Stir in ricotta, Parmesan and parsley.

3. To assemble casserole, spread 2 cups lasagna sauce to cover bottom of pan. Place half of cooked rigatoni over sauce; top with half of ricotta mixture, dropped by spoonfuls. Layer with 1 cup mozzarella, 2 cups lasagna sauce, remaining rigatoni and ricotta mixture. Top with 1 cup mozzarella, remaining lasagna sauce and remaining 1 cup mozzarella.

4. Cover with foil and bake 60 to 70 minutes or until bubbly. Uncover and continue cooking about 5 minutes or until cheese is melted. Let stand 15 minutes before serving.

Sunny Day Casserole

Creamy Chicken and Pasta with Spinach

Makes 8 servings

  6 ounces uncooked egg noodles
  1 tablespoon olive oil
  ¼ cup chopped onion
  ¼ cup chopped red bell pepper
  1 package (10 ounces) frozen spinach, thawed and drained
  2 boneless skinless chicken breasts (¾ pound), cooked and cut into 1-inch pieces
  1 can (4 ounces) sliced mushrooms, drained
  2 cups (8 ounces) shredded Swiss cheese
  1 container (8 ounces) sour cream
  ¾ cup half-and-half
  2 eggs, lightly beaten
  ½ teaspoon salt
  Red onion and fresh spinach for garnish

1. Preheat oven to 350°F. Prepare noodles according to package directions; set aside. Spray 13×9-inch baking dish with nonstick cooking spray; set aside.

2. Heat oil in large skillet over medium-high heat. Add onion and bell pepper; cook and stir 2 minutes or until onion is tender. Add spinach, chicken, mushrooms and cooked noodles; stir to combine.

3. Combine cheese, sour cream, half-and-half, eggs and salt in medium bowl; blend well.

4. Add cheese mixture to chicken mixture; stir to combine. Pour into prepared baking dish. Bake, covered, 30 to 35 minutes or until heated through. Garnish with red onion and fresh spinach, if desired.

Barbecue Chicken with Cornbread Topper

Makes 8 servings

  1½ pounds boneless skinless chicken breasts and thighs
  1 can (15 ounces) red beans, rinsed and drained
  1 can (8 ounces) tomato sauce
  1 cup chopped green bell pepper
  ½ cup barbecue sauce
  1 package (6.5 ounces) cornbread mix
  Ingredients to prepare cornbread mix

1. Cut chicken into ¾-inch cubes. Heat nonstick skillet over medium heat. Add chicken; cook and stir 5 minutes or until cooked through.

2. Combine chicken, beans, tomato sauce, bell pepper and barbecue sauce in 8-inch microwavable ovenproof dish.

3. Preheat oven to 375°F. Loosely cover chicken mixture with plastic wrap or waxed paper. Microwave at MEDIUM-HIGH (70% power) 8 minutes or until heated through, stirring after 4 minutes.

4. While chicken mixture is heating, prepare cornbread mix according to package directions. Spoon batter over chicken mixture. Bake 15 to 18 minutes or until toothpick inserted in center of cornbread layer comes out clean.

Cheddar and Leek Strata

Makes 12 servings

>   8 **eggs, lightly beaten**
>   2 **cups milk**
>   ½ **cup ale or beer**
>   2 **cloves garlic, minced**
>   ¼ **teaspoon salt**
>   ¼ **teaspoon black pepper**
>   1 **loaf (16 ounces) sourdough bread, cut into ½-inch cubes**
>   2 **small leeks, coarsely chopped**
>   1 **red bell pepper, chopped**
>   1½ **cups (6 ounces) shredded Swiss cheese**
>   1½ **cups (6 ounces) shredded sharp Cheddar cheese**
>   **Fresh sage sprigs for garnish**

1. Combine eggs, milk, ale, garlic, salt and black pepper in large bowl. Beat until well blended.

2. Place ½ of bread cubes on bottom of greased 13×9-inch baking dish. Sprinkle ½ of leeks and ½ of bell pepper over bread cubes. Top with ¾ cup Swiss cheese and ¾ cup Cheddar cheese. Repeat layers with remaining ingredients, ending with Cheddar cheese.

3. Pour egg mixture evenly over top. Cover tightly with plastic wrap or foil. Weigh top of strata down with slightly smaller baking dish. Refrigerate strata at least 2 hours or overnight.

4. Preheat oven to 350°F. Bake, uncovered, 40 to 45 minutes or until center is set. Garnish with fresh sage, if desired. Serve immediately.

Patchwork Casserole

Makes 8 to 10 servings

- 2 **pounds ground beef**
- 2 **cups chopped green bell pepper**
- 1 **cup chopped onion**
- 2 **pounds frozen Southern-style hash brown potatoes, thawed**
- 2 **cans (8 ounces each) tomato sauce**
- 1 **cup water**
- 1 **can (6 ounces) tomato paste**
- 1 **teaspoon salt**
- ½ **teaspoon dried basil, crumbled**
- ¼ **teaspoon black pepper**
- 1 **pound pasteurized process American cheese, thinly sliced**

1. Preheat oven to 350°F.

2. Brown beef in large skillet over medium heat about 10 minutes; drain off fat. Add bell pepper and onion; cook and stir until tender, about 4 minutes. Stir in potatoes, tomato sauce, water, tomato paste, salt, basil and black pepper.

3. Spoon half of mixture into 13×9×2-inch baking pan or 3-quart baking dish; top with half of cheese. Spoon remaining meat mixture evenly on top of cheese. Cover pan with aluminum foil. Bake 45 minutes.

4. Cut remaining cheese into decorative shapes; place on top of casserole. Let stand loosely covered until cheese melts, about 5 minutes.

Patchwork Casserole

Hungarian Goulash Casserole

Make 4 to 6 servings

- 1 pound ground pork
- ¼ teaspoon salt
- ¼ teaspoon ground nutmeg
- ¼ teaspoon black pepper
- 1 tablespoon vegetable oil
- 1 cup reduced-fat sour cream, divided
- 1 tablespoon cornstarch
- 1 can (10¾ ounces) cream of celery soup
- 1 cup milk
- 1 teaspoon sweet Hungarian paprika
- 1 package (12 ounces) egg noodles, cooked and drained
- 2 teaspoons minced fresh dill (optional)

1. Preheat oven to 325°F. Spray 13×9-inch casserole dish with nonstick cooking spray.

2. Combine pork, salt, nutmeg and pepper in bowl. Shape into 1-inch meatballs. Heat oil in large skillet over medium-high heat. Add meatballs. Cook 10 minutes or until browned on all sides and no longer pink in center. Remove meatballs from skillet; discard drippings.

3. Stir together ¼ cup sour cream and cornstarch in small bowl. Spoon into same skillet. Add remaining ¾ cup sour cream, soup, milk and paprika. Stir until smooth.

4. Spoon cooked noodles into prepared dish. Arrange meatballs over noodles and cover with sauce. Bake 20 minutes or until hot. Sprinkle with dill, if desired.

Hungarian Goulash Casserole

Creamy Chicken & Vegetables with Puff Pastry

Makes 6 servings

- 2 whole chicken breasts, split (about 2 pounds)
- 1 medium onion, sliced
- 4 carrots, coarsely chopped, divided
- 4 ribs celery with leaves, cut into 1-inch pieces, divided
- 1 frozen puff pastry sheet, thawed
- 2 tablespoons butter or margarine
- 1 medium onion, chopped
- ½ pound fresh mushrooms, sliced
- ½ cup all-purpose flour
- 1 teaspoon dried basil leaves
- 1 teaspoon salt
- ¼ to ½ teaspoon white pepper
- 1 cup milk
- 1 cup frozen peas, thawed

1. To make chicken stock, place chicken, sliced onion, ⅓ of carrots and ⅓ of celery in Dutch oven. Add enough cold water to cover. Cover and bring to a boil over medium heat. Reduce heat to low. Simmer 5 to 7 minutes or until chicken is no longer pink in center.

2. Remove chicken; cool. Strain stock through large sieve lined with several layers of dampened cheesecloth; discard vegetables. Refrigerate stock; skim off any fat that forms on top. Measure 2 cups stock.

3. When chicken is cool enough to handle, remove skin and bones; discard. Cut chicken into bite-size pieces.

4. Place remaining carrots, celery and enough water to cover in medium saucepan. Cover; bring to a boil. Reduce heat to medium-low; simmer 8 minutes or until vegetables are crisp-tender. Set aside.

5. Preheat oven to 400°F. Roll puff pastry out on lightly floured surface to 12×8-inch rectangle. Place on ungreased baking sheet; bake 15 minutes. Set aside.

6. Melt butter in large saucepan over medium heat. Add chopped onion and mushrooms; cook and stir 5 minutes or until tender. Stir in flour, basil, salt and pepper. Pour in reserved chicken stock and milk. Cook until mixture begins to boil. Cook 1 minute longer, stirring constantly.

7. Stir in reserved chicken, peas, carrots and celery. Cook until heated through. Pour mixture into 12×8-inch baking dish. Top with puff pastry; bake 5 minutes longer until heated through. Garnish as desired.

Creamy Chicken & Vegetables with Puff Pastry

Easy Tuna & Pasta Pot Pie

Makes 5 servings

- 1 tablespoon margarine or butter
- 1 large onion, chopped
- 1½ cups cooked small shell pasta or elbow macaroni
- 1 can (10¾ ounces) condensed cream of celery or mushroom soup, undiluted
- 1 cup frozen peas, thawed
- 1 can (6 ounces) tuna in water, drained and flaked into pieces
- ½ cup sour cream
- ½ teaspoon dried dill weed
- ¼ teaspoon salt
- 1 package (7.5 ounces) buttermilk or country biscuits

1. Preheat oven to 400°F. Melt margarine in medium ovenproof skillet over medium heat. Add onion; cook 5 minutes, stirring occasionally.

2. Stir in pasta, soup, peas, tuna, sour cream, dill and salt; mix well. Cook 3 minutes or until hot. Press mixture down in skillet to form even layer.

3. Unwrap biscuit dough; arrange individual biscuits over tuna mixture. Bake 15 minutes or until biscuits are golden brown and tuna mixture is bubbly.

Acknowledgments

The publisher would like to thank the companies and organizations listed below for the use of their recipes and photographs in this publication.

Barilla America, Inc.

Bob Evans®

Florida Department of Agriculture and Consumer Services, Bureau of Seafood and Aquaculture

Hillshire Farm®

Reckitt Benckiser Inc.

Unilever Bestfoods North America